Shifting The
Mind To Manifest
What You Want

· ·

Angie Clark

**RICK
AQUA**

SHIFTING THE MIND TO MANIFEST WHAT YOU WANT

ANGIE CLARK

Graphic Design By:
Rick Aqua

Shifting The Mind To Manifest What You Want

Copyright © Angie Clark 2020

ISBN: 978-1-73455-760-2

Angie Clark Publishing Rockford, Illinois

DEDICATIONS

This is written as a guide for those who wants to break free in the mind may you be free indeed.

CONTENT

INTRODUCTION

CHAPTER 1   SELF LOVE

CHAPTER 2   BEING PRESENT IN THE NOW

CHAPTER 3   LETTING GO OF PAST PAINS AND
                 FORGIVING THE PAST

CHAPTER 4   TRAINING THE MIND TO BE
                 POSITIVE

CHAPTER 5   TESTIMONIALS/ TRUE STORY
                 CONFESSIONS

CHAPTER 6   HELPFUL TIPS INVOLVING
                 AFFFIRMATIONS AND
                 MANIFESTATIONS

CHAPTER 7   AFFIRMATIONS OF POSITIVITY

CHAPTER 8   THE GREAT I AM

CHAPTER 9   GREATFUL DECLARATION

CHAPTER 10   AFFIRMATIONS OF WHOLENESS AND
                 LOVE

CHAPTER 11   AFFIRMATIONS OF LETTING GO

CHAPTER 12   PROTECTING ENERGY
                 AFFIRMATIONS

CHAPTER 13   AFFIRMATIONS OF HEALTH

CHAPTER 14   THE JOURNALS/ REFLECTIONS

INTRODUCTION

In today's' society we have been conditioned to think a certain way through home, school and social media. It is through these avenues of interacting with others we learn what is acceptable valuable and important. This can have a dangerous effect on a persons' mind by disabling them to think for themselves. This also causes limitations on a persons' reasoning for themselves which is known as social conditioning. Once a person is aware of this controlled mindset and desire to think for themselves, this marks the beginning of an awakening. This awakening will bring a person to want to shift their mind to think of what it is they really want out of life. Within this book we will discuss solutions and resolutions that will help manifest what you want such as being present in the now through meditation, being positive, letting go of past pains and hurts, forgiving the past and by saying positive affirmations and declarations.

CHAPTER 1
SELF LOVE

What is self love? Self love is genuine appreciation of self. It is the appreciation of who you are, your talents, your gifts, and your natural self. Respecting yourself in behavior and through speech. Self love is when you set healthy limits and boundaries with others. It is being protective of self by not disclosing of your private and personal matters. It is trusting and believing in yourself. It is confidently being sure and grounded within self. These are all acts of self love. Many of us were unfortunate of being taught as a child how to love ourselves properly, while others were. This was due to parents who did not know how to love themselves because they were not taught the importance of self love. This led to another generation of lack mindfulness of self love. The key to breaking the chains of lack of self love is to know that self love is the basis and essence of Life. One must love themselves to successfully thrive in life and productively interact with others. In order for one to have a healthy well being and prosperous life one must love self. The way you see and treat yourself is the same way others will see and treat you, therefore it is wise to see and treat yourself in a positive light. Loving yourself teaches others how to treat you as well. If someone sees that you have low self esteem others will be prone to treat you with lesser value. They maybe even be prone to take advantage of you. So if you want others to respect you for who you are learn to love and respect yourself first. Always strive on improving and enhancing yourself for it is important for building self confidence, self esteem and inner strength. If you struggle with having self love now is the time to start focusing on your goodness, your strengths, your skills. Try focusing more on the goodness of yourself without criticism. Criticism can cloud the mind with negative thoughts one after the other. Its alright to see where you can improve in something but it is not alright to focus on how bad something felt because it can cause overthinking and feelings of inadequacy or lack. If you do see a fault within yourself, it is a good thing because you are presented with the chance to address and change that aspect of yourself that needs to be altered. If we are honest with ourselves we can gain great solution for ourselves. Improving ourselves is self love too. Anything that has to do with becoming a better version of ourselves in a positive way is self love. It is our responsibility to love on ourselves. No one can do it for you. Without it expect for your life to be incomplete or unfulfilled. Love of self feels good and the more you actively participate in activities that demonstrates self love the more empowered you will feel from within. Your self esteem and self worthiness will blossom and mature within you. This growth and clarity should be so life transforming that you will want to continue to invest in self and love on yourself like you know you deserve. You can read all the books on self improvement and listen to other peoples life stories of how they learned to love themselves, but until you try it for yourself, you will not get to experience this process of progression. Self love is a way of life, something you do for a lifetime, one day at a time.

CHAPTER 2
BEING PRESENT IN THE NOW

We are so bombarded with thoughts and memories of our past as well as thoughts of our future. Thoughts of what our last conversation was about with a loved one or a friend. Even thoughts of errands we have to do tomorrow runs across our minds. Sometimes we even become so preoccupied with all sorts of random thoughts that we forget to be in the present moment of now. A person can be sweeping the floor yet their mind will all of a sudden drift off to thinking of something totally different. If we focus much on our future sometimes it can bring feelings of anxiety and if we focus much on our past it can allow feelings of regret and resentment. Our goal should be focused on the present moment of now. Being in the present moment of now brings us a sense of calmness and peace of mind. A familiar way of engaging ourselves in becoming present in the now is thru meditation. Meditation is a technique practiced to achieve a calm clear state of mind. One way to begin is to focus on breathing. Try and find a comfortable place to sit and be still. Close your eyes and begin to focus your attention on your breathing. Breath in to where you can feel your breath come in as you inhale and where you feel your breath go out as you exhale. Continue to do this a few times until you feel relaxed within the mind and body and soul. As thoughts come in allow them to leave without entertaining them. This may seem tough to attain at first but be patient and allow the thoughts to come and go and fade out. Simply began to focus on your senses and begin to feel. Lay your hands on your laps relaxed or on whatever is near. What does it feel like? What is the texture? Is it soft or hard? Next begin to listen. What do you hear? Is it quiet or loud? What do you smell? Are the smells unfamiliar or pleasant. Now think of the taste in your mouth. Is there tastes of minty peppermint or simply the familiar taste of your

mouths' saliva? What do you see? Are there people places or

things around you? Are you indoors in a quiet room or at a park

sitting in the grass while the sun shines on you? Focus on the

senses of touch, taste, smell, sight and hearing. Focusing on the

senses are great ways to become present in the moment. There are

other ways of becoming present in the now, these are only a few

suggestions. Some people may become present and calm when

near water like the ocean or a lake while others may find that

taking a salt water bath with candle light helps them to unwind

and relax. Some may ride in a vehicle while the wind blows on

their face soothes them and brings them in the present moment.

Listening to a favorite song that gives a sense of joy and

pleasantness is another way to become present. Working with the

energy of stones and absorbing its effects is another way to

become present. For the grown and mature sex can be a tool of

becoming present to release tension or stress build up. It varies

for everyone. In the pursuit of our busy days it is important to take a few moments to become centered and present in the moment. The more you practice this the more it will become easier to do. The ability to unwind and take on a calmer state of mind will become natural.

CHAPTER 3
LETTING GO OF PAST PAINS AND FORGIVING THE PAST

At some times in our lives we will all encounter moments with other people that can be unpleasant to us. From our childhood and on throughout our adult lives we continuously encounter moments of happiness as well as unpleasant ones. Sometimes we take the not so pleasant moments to heart and hold on to the way it made us feel. We relive those feelings again in our mind. Some of those feelings were low in vibration such as anger, sadness, resentfulness, unforgiveness, despair, anxiety, depression, abandonment, rejection, neglect and even insecurities.

As we entertain those feelings and the unpleasant memories it effects us by keeping us stuck and stagnant unable to release it and move on. When we do this we block new opportunities to manifest growth and expansion in our lives. This can result in our happiness being altered in a negative way. Any future relationship we develop will also be negatively affected due to unreleased issues of our past. It is unfortunate to know that holding to the pains and hurts of our past as well as not forgiving results in ruin and spoil. It results in ruin and spoil because it affects the potential for healthy well being within self as well as in relationships. It is easier said than done to forgive others but it is something we all should consider and practice. The more you forgive yourself and others the easier it will be to let go and be free within. This does not mean that when others hurt or offend us it will be automatic to forgive them and not be affected. What it does mean is that forgiveness will allow us to move past the negativity of dealing with others who may hurt or offend us. It will make us more aware that when other people hurt or offend us that we need to release those emotions because if not it will begin

to hinder us. It can hinder us in developing bitterness

resentfulness, negative mind set, grudges and disharmony within

ourselves. The way to release these feelings is through

forgiveness and making peace with the issue. Forgiveness is

accepting what has occurred, good or bad because we cannot

change the past, but we can move on from it without harsh

judgments. Sometimes forgiving others even if they do not ask for

your forgiveness is needed to clear your mind. A key to forgiving

is to have a open mind in knowing we are human and we make

mistakes. No one is perfect and we hurt others sometimes

without even being aware of it. Another way to look towards

forgiveness is to know that sometimes pain causes us to grow and

mature. Pain can teach valuable lessons that pleasure cannot. The

truth is that we learn lessons of boundaries and limitations from

pain. Lessons of maturity and awareness is what pain brings as

well. Pain wakes us up where we were asleep. Forgiving

ourselves is knowing that we are imperfect and always learning moment by moment. Sometimes we offend others without knowing as well. In remembering that we all make mistakes and are prone to offend others at times helps us to understand that misunderstandings and differences in opinion will occur. The question is how do we react after the damage is done? Do we allow offenses and pain from others to paralyze and traumatize us forever or do we see the lessons to be learned from it and move on? If we choose to learn from those experiences, forgive the situation and move on, we liberate ourselves. We liberate ourselves and heal from those experiences. Healing and liberation are the benefits of letting go of past pains and forgiving our past.

CHAPTER 4

TRAINING THE MIND TO BE POSITIVE

Training the mind to be positive can be a challenge especially if one is prone to focus more on the negative side of things. One way to be positive in a positive mindset is to be thankful and grateful. Being grateful for your current state of being, loved ones, and for what you have will bring a pleasant state of mind. One way to become grateful for your current state of being is to think of someone else who is less fortunate than yourself. Think of how someone else is not as fortunate to have the things you have and live the life you are living. We have so much to be grateful for yet we take so much for granted. Whenever you feel yourself drifting off into melancholy just think of how your situation could be worse. Imagine your life now without the people places and things that exists in your life. What about your health and well being? Think of how it would feel to be in poor health. These thoughts and reflections should bring us

to a state of humility and gratefulness. As we reflect and take into

account all of the things that are beneficial to our well being, a

sense of gratitude will come upon us because we are reminded

that without those things and people and places in our lives we

would be in a less fortunate state of being. Another suggestion

would be to find the humor in every circumstance and situation

you find yourself in. Pay attention to the light side of things.

When you focus more on the positive in a situation you will

attract more positive to yourself. The thoughts we think and feel

attracts to us more of them. If your thoughts are mostly negative

you will attract more of that. So being aware of your thoughts can

benefit you because then you will have the option to entertain the

positive thoughts or the negative thoughts. It is a choice.

Remember your choices will set the tone for your outcome.

Entertaining negative thoughts will attract negative vibes,

encounters, and outcomes. The key is to be mindful of what you

are thinking. When you control your thoughts you control your entire life. How you react to life is what will determine your entire existence. It is simple. If you respond to life negatively that is exactly what you mirror back to yourself. Just as well as if your response to life is positive that is exactly what you will mirror back to yourself. Continue to stay aware of your thoughts as often as you can. If you see that you are prone to thinking mostly negative thoughts, simply switch your thoughts on something positive which will attract more goodness. It is that simple.

CHAPTER 5
TESTIMONIALS/ TRUE STORY CONFESSIONS

There was a time in my life where I came to the realization that all of the hard core negative circumstances I experienced in my lifetime was to strengthen and mold me into a better version of myself. Those deep seated uncomfortable pains I endured were all lessons I needed to learn. I can remember looking back at those times in my life of sadness from a victim point of view. My mind felt so limited and my judgment was clouded. I was unable to grasp why I kept making decisions that hindered me in the long run. I always wondered why most of my relationships fell apart. I recall the tears of frustrations and the agony I felt deep within my heart weighing heavy. The things I use to find pleasure and relief in no longer gave me pleasure nor relief. I was met with even deeper depths of despair, being overwhelmed and of sadness. I fell into a depressed state of being. Feeling sorry for myself and having a pity party. I was drowning in misery, regret and hopelessness. I slept so much that when I tried to sleep I was unable to. I found myself wide awake forced to face my raw reality. I cried a lot on a daily basis. I prayed desperately unto The Divine for help. I would ask to be rid of this dark reality I found myself in by allowing me to pass away in my sleep. Yes I was hoping to pass away in my sleep to another realm other than my current one. Days passed as I woke up in the morning unable

to escape in my sleep. So now my prayers changed from escapism to prayers of helping me to cope with my emotions. I needed strength to face my reality. I wanted to heal because I was wounded deeply from within. I wanted healing, but was clueless as to how to heal properly. So I continued to ask The Divine for day by day for help and divine intervention on my behalf. Days passed and I felt a little better than the day before. Meditation and prayer became my constant source of strength and healing. I was patient with myself and pampered myself more. I took small steps towards overcoming my issues. I took my focus off of all the things that brought me sadness and occupied my time with positive activities. I studied topics that I had always been curious about. As I did this my mind shifted away from my issues and onto the positive of my new life that was unfolding before my eyes. I heard about the laws of attraction and how the sayings of positive affirmations can change your life for the better. I also heard how the repetitive sayings of positive affirmations can train the mind to become positive and to manifest what you desire. I was very curious as to how true this was. In my spare time I listened to people who spoke life giving words of wisdom and healing. I found a sense of peace from visiting my brother at his place. Visiting his place gave me a calm peace of mind. Laughing and talking with my brother felt genuinely good as respect and love flowed between us. At the same time I was interacting with a brother from another country who inspired and encouraged my heart beyond measure. This brother literally spoke words of life into me. He had an enormous impact on me in a real way. Both of these brothers were instrumental to my healing whether they knew it or not. As time progressed I felt light at heart as my spirit uplifted. My mind was clearer and sharper no longer clouded or confused. My inner strength increased. I found enjoyment in becoming more active physically. My healing was in full effect in all areas of my life. I kept a journal and only wrote in it when I felt prompted to do so. My writings included short prayers of gratitude and appreciation, positive affirmations of how I felt about myself and how I wanted to feel. My notebook filled up over time. I would reread the things I wrote and was well pleased with them. At times I would read them aloud and believed in what I was saying. Feelings of gratitude, joy, pleasure, and happiness filled my mind body and soul. It seemed like I had tapped in another realm of awareness and wisdom. I felt like I had awakened from a nightmare and was safe again. That nightmare represented the limited mindset and reality I had previously been living in. I resumed my days as usual and was met with clear visuals of a better version of myself. Seeing these visuals gave me great motivation to work towards making these visuals my reality.

To know I can create my reality from my thoughts along with my efforts gave me relief. I was astonished at the simplicity of it. I became more aware in seeing the good in all situations I was faced in. I was overall occupied with becoming a happier better version of myself. Certain people naturally became drawn to me and wanted to be in my company. Family members and friends that were connected to me on a deeper level grew closer to me. Opposing associates and family members fell away from me naturally without a struggle. Somehow we seemed to grow apart without question. I was empowered with a new sense of security within myself which I had never experienced before. I actually saw the positive affirmations I said occur in my life. I knew for myself that it is true that saying and believing the affirmations will manifest into your life. The law of attraction really exists because I tried it for myself and found it to be true. In my leisure time I was drawn to go back to enjoying the things I did for fun as a child like: coloring ,writing, drawing, braiding hair on a doll and dancing to music. As a child, these were the activities I engaged myself in. These activities gave me a sense of pleasure and allowed my creativity to flow freely. I enjoyed my own company more without looking for external people places and things to entertain me. I experienced so many epiphanies as I grew in ascension. My mind expanded and took me places I never even knew existed. Everyday of my life was an exciting new one because of my optimistic mindset. I expected miracles to take place and surprises, big and small did occur. I welcomed each day as a gift and was anticipating its arrival. Even on days when unfortunate events occurred I saw the good that came out of it. I acknowledged a lot about myself like my faults within me that were hidden or that I was in denial of. I saw the self sabotage and hindrances I was causing myself. Seeing these issues in myself caused me to take inventory and improve self. I made it a daily task to work on improving my defaults within self. The more I did this the more I saw the impact I had on others. I saw how I was becoming a beacon of light for others. I realized in order for me to remain a positive force in others lives I needed to tear down within myself those things that interfered with my growth

healing, abundance, success and happiness. I searched myself and

went deep within through prayer and meditation as I listened to

my inner voice of truth. My intuition heightened and gave me the

answers I was seeking. My intuition whispered to me truths about

myself that exposed me naked. It exposed to me how I was self

sabotaging myself by my thoughts and perspectives that kept me

in a negative state of mind from my youth. From my upbringing I

was conditioned by default to think and focus on the negativity of

life. I was not taught how to heal from the hard knocks of life.

Nor was I taught to be happy from within. I honestly was ignorant

to the fact of how to manifest starting with my thoughts. Most

things in my life were incomplete. For example, I would start new

projects in my life and rarely would I complete them to the end. I

lacked motivation and drive. I mostly did what was required in

life to survive. I was guilty of lacking motivation needed to push

myself above and beyond. I was operating from a lack mindset of

poverty. I lacked self love, self confidence, and self esteem. I needed to change within because the quality of my life was limited. I produced incomplete, immature results in my life which kept me in a stagnant and limited reality. Now I was faced to choose whether I wanted to continue in this poor quality reality or choose a life of healing growth and stability. I chose a life of healing growth and stability. No matter the the work I needed to put in I was willing to take action in thinking positive, being more grateful in attitude towards life, and accepting myself, people,

places and things as they are. I desired the ability to flow with life and not against it. I was willing to change my thoughts, my speech, my conduct and my interactions with others. I was practical in knowing this would be a life journey process developing moment by moment. This would not happen over night. I was aware that this would take me through a transformation of deep healing and deep cleansing. I was realistic in welcoming all aspects of life, whether it be pleasant or unfortunate, I was ready to face it. I underwent a grand transformation on all levels perceivable. I came out refined for good evolving and growing at a substantial rate. Truly there is no gain without pain. We must experience darkness to appreciate the light. When we welcome the ups and downs of life we have a balanced and healthy view of life. Accepting all aspects of life is beneficial because it allows us to face each situation with ease void of anxiety. Enjoy your life as it unfolds moment by moment because life is a gift.

CHAPTER 6

HELPFUL TIPS IN INVOLVING AFFIRMATIONS AND

MANIFESTATIONS

There are rules to manifesting what it is you desire. The first step is to make the intention of what it is you desire. Be as specific and clear as possible when setting your intentions. Imagine what it looks like. What does it feel like? What does it sound like? What does it smell like? What does it taste like?

Feel as though you already have what it is you desire. As you use your senses to determine your desires a sense of joy, contentment, and happiness should arise within yourself. Say out of your mouth and speak into existence your desires by believing it. Believe what you are saying is true. Start to view and visualize your desires in your mind. Own it as if it is already yours. Trust that it will one day show up in your reality. Continue to stay optimistic and hopeful. Make actions that support your desires by doing what you can in the physical to bring your desires into your life. Be patient by allowing your desires to flow to you in divine timing. Enjoy the practice and process of manifesting. Always be aware of your thoughts because they create your words and your words create your reality. Being mindful and aware of your thoughts are important to combat negativity. We all want to

incorporate goodness into our lives so we must stay in a positive mindset to do so. Thinking positive, speaking positive and acting in a positive manner all will attract goodness back to ourselves.

Remember to allow thoughts to come and fade away. Entertain the positive thoughts while giving less attention to the negative ones. Whatever is good, lovely, positive, beautiful, pleasing and of good rapport, think on those things for it will surely show up in your reality. As you read the affirmations you will find the desire to create your own more personalized affirmations and

declarations. Feel free to do so because each affirmation is very personal to each individual. The affirmations and declarations in this book are ones that were particularly impressive upon myself. I was compelled to share these affirmations because they have enhanced my mindset in a major way. May they have a positive impression upon you as well.

CHAPTER 7

AFFIRMATIONS OF POSITIVITY

Today I give thanks for the gift of life

I am grateful for all that I have experienced and the growth I have gained from those experiences

I am spirit having a human experience

I love believe and trust in myself now more than ever before

I am loved lovable and loving

I am balanced in my mind body and soul

I am hopeful and optimistic

I am patient with myself

I am secure and sure within myself

I am worthy of goodness

I know who I am

I am greatness and I expect nothing less of myself but greatness

I am the best of my kind

I stand in my power and in my truth

I am focused and disciplined and sure of myself

I take on a positive mindset, positive attitude, and positive perspective as I face each day

I am realistic and practical

I am calm peaceful and graceful even in the face of adversity

I am patient when challenges arise

I am flexible and adaptable as I flow with the waves of life

I am humorous and light in heart as I face each opportunity in my life

I am ready for whatever as I face life with grace

I am true to myself as I set healthy boundaries with people places and things

I see people places and things as they are and not as I wish them to be

I go within to seek healing guidance and wisdom

I am careful with my thoughts because they create my words and my words create my reality

My words are healing as I speak words of life

I listen to my intuition more as it guides and warns me for it is my inner voice of truth

I turn stress anxiety and nervousness into excitement

I am determined as I keep my focus on love light and the spiritual aspects of life

I trust and believe all that I need is being supplied by the universe in divine timing

I give my fears and concerns about my material and financial issues to my angels for healing and transmutation

I give and receive with gratitude

I dream my desires as they become my reality

My thoughts vibrations and energy are in alignment with my dreams desires goals and purposes

My genius talents and gifts are fully activated and used for the highest good

My wishes are commanded

As I use my skills talents and gifts to its fullest extent I attract to me all of my hearts' desire

I am attuned with my life purpose

I fulfill my life purpose

CHAPTER 8

THE GREAT I AM

I am in sync with my divine self

I am that I am

I am : Graceful Majestic Gracious Fearless Jovial Bountiful

Limitless Courageous Magical Clever Initiative Dynamic Healthy

Patient Lovable Sexy Attractive Gentle Devotional Creative

Charismatic Pleasant Humorous Discerning Inquisitive Curious

Happy Comfortable Calm Miraculous Desirable Stable Balanced

Fair Structured Wise Energetic Whole Focused Wealthy

Electrifying Inspiring Intuitive Natural Harmonious Favored

Awesome Mobile Worthy Invigorating Responsible Responsive

to truth Receptive to truth and open to receive all that is mine by

divine right

So be it

The Great I Am

CHAPTER 9
GRATEFUL DECLARATION

I am thankful unto the Divine for assisting me in uplifting my vibrations where I live in a new timeline full of joy freedom bliss unconditional love and happiness. I ask that strength support guidance and fortification be mine. Bestow upon me infinite abundance by clearing my old past time lines of grief sadness betrayal abuse and depression while transmuting those energies into stamina endurance and perseverance as I journey on in life victoriously.

So be it

CHAPTER 10

AFFIRMATIONS OF WHOLENESS AND LOVE

I am in love with my natural self. I am in love with my natural

essence,talents, gifts, genius, cells, skin,hair,body without make

up to define who I am. I am infinite beauty born naked free and

complete I am. I embody all that is mine by divine right. I now

embody and manifest ascension, awareness, awakening

activation, patience, wisdom, love, knowledge of self, focus,

groundedness, abundant life, prosperity, discipline, motivation,

action, stability, self sufficiency, inspiration, success, victory,

knowledge, aligned chakras, self love, wealth, good health,

power, discernment, unforeseen new avenues of monetary

abundance. I embody a positive mindset. My creative essence and

genius helps me to realize my dreams and desires. I am stable

balanced and in harmony with myself. My feminine and

masculine self are harmoniously in sync fueled by divine purpose

I am full of inspiration and creativity at all times flowing freely

My life is a beautiful surprise

My life is miraculous

My life is gaining focus,momentum, structure and balance

I am expecting miracles to take form in my reality

I utilize my time productively

I can do all things because I believe and trust in my higher self

I am paid in full from my natural talents and gifts

I live my life in modesty

Blockages and barriers in my mind are cleared and healed allowing me to think clearly

Blockages and barriers in my life are cleared out allowing me to flow freely in my essence

I am granted all my hearts desires welcoming their arrival

I take action daily towards my goals and desires

I take action daily to awaken my personal power

I excel in progression

I accelerate in high frequencies

I am actively courageous and energetic

My vibrations and frequency align with my life purposes

I call those things which are not as though they are into existence

I create I birth and I manifest into existence all that I desire and daydream of

I use my charisma to bring to me my desires

I take what I was given in life and make the best out of it

I believe in my dreams so much that it has no choice but to manifest into my reality

I am in high demand and well sought after for the natural flow of my talents and gifts within me

All things work together for my good because I love myself and the Most High

I recognize the positive impact I have on others lives

I listen to my intuition more than ever before

I receive because I believe

Avalanches of abundance descend upon me now as I receive openly effortlessly and easily with grace

The love of The Most High within me now draws to me all that I need to keep me happy whole and

 complete as I walk daily in divine love

The love of The Most High within me draws to me my true soul mate and beloved one to me

I call in and attract my tribe to me

I enjoy healthy relationships and friendships with my soul tribe

Issues between my family and loved ones are sorted and resolved to the advantage of all involved

I welcome new and genuine friendships to enter my life for growth and expansion

I am friendly

I welcome true and real love to enter my life

I so much love myself

I open my heart as I experience unconditional love on levels like never before

My mind body and soul are in harmony

My mind body and soul are lively energetic and in a steady flow

I am emotionally balanced

I am fearlessly and wonderfully made

I seek my purposes in this lifetime

I focus my logical mind to make smart effective business decisions

CHAPTER 11

AFFIRMATIONS OF LETTING GO

Any part of my soul that I gave away in sin I now call back unto me healed restored and energized

As an act of my free will I choose to loose any darkness any fear any pride any impatience any strife any bitterness any unforgiveness any anger any resentfulness any jealousy any offense any disease any doubt any laziness any poverty any lack any lust any barrenness any chaos any rebelliousness to truth any disrespect any addictions any arrogance any envy anything less than love I loose these from my mind body and soul So be it

I now call back unto me any parts of my soul that has been fragmented due to others crashing through my boundary walls with shock trauma anger and abuse of all kind be healed restored and replenished

I thank you Father God for loving me more than my earthly father could

I thank you Mother God for loving me more than my earthly mother could

I let go of any fears as I welcome support from my spirit guides angels and ancestors

I let go of childhood trauma painful experiences and their negative effects it has placed upon my life

I am covered and guided by ancestors and spirit guides

I let go of fears of abandonment negligence and rejection

I let go of obsessive and possessive behaviors

All cords of addictions are severed in my life

I move away from a victim mentality as I take responsibility for my life

I let go of control issues as I allow people places and things to be as they are

I let go of people places things that no longer serve me as I welcome people places and things that serve my highest good

I let go of negative attitudes,perspectives,mindsets,thinking,train of thoughts and beliefs that no longer serve me as I take on a healthy attitude, perspective, mindset, thinking, train of thoughts and belief that serve my highest good

I am free of the spirit of lack and barrenness as I am abundant and fruitful in all my ways

I let go of sadness depression barrenness oppression and lack as I welcome joy gladness gratitude fertility optimism and abundance unto myself

I let go of negativity and doubt as I take on a positive spirit of belief and trust in myself

I let go of distractions, confusion, and chaos as I become clear,focused and peaceful within

I let go of false beliefs of love and relationships

I free myself of trying to change others

I let go of titles and labels of people and treat each individual according to their actions

I let go of laziness and procrastination as I take action towards my goals and aspirations

I let go of negative thoughts of myself as I think more pleasant thoughts of myself

I let go of limited perceptions of myself as I become more aware that I am limitless

I free myself and all involved from past hurts and pains as we become free to move into new experiences

I let go of fear based beliefs and perceptions that blocks truth

CHAPTER 12

PROTECTING ENERGY AFFIRMATIONS

I invoke the I am GOD presence in me now

I am free, safe and light

I welcome positive energy and positive vibes in my life

I radiate with strength courage and power from within

My vibrations and frequencies are strong

I am surrounded by joy and love

Love and light fuels my DNA

I am shielded from all forms of negative projections from others

As I rest I am protected from all harm

I am protected wherever I am by The Divine

I am unbothered from lower vibrations

My highest self protects me from all things less than love

I am unbothered from negative curses and hexes for I am divinely protected

I am free from all energetic trauma and generational denominational curses in my DNA

Any weapons formed against me returns back to its sender void

I make it through the storms and trials of life victoriously

I transmute all negative energy projected onto me and within me into positive love and light for healing

I call upon earth, air, fire, ether, spirit and water to assist me along my journey

I am always attracting positive people who assist me in achieving my soul purpose

I call upon my angels and spirit guides to sever all cords of demonic ties that I have become attached to be loosed now

I am free of self sabotage

I demolish the strongholds in my mind that brings despair, blockages and lack

I am free of restrictions and chains holding me back from moving forward

CHAPTER 13

AFFIRMATIONS OF HEALTH

My health is my wealth

I love my body internally and externally

I am well

I am grateful for my healthy body

I am thankful to be alive

I am thankful for the healing in my body

My body is completely healthy now

I am strong energetic and vibrant

The cells in my body are healthy and active

My body heals itself easily and rapidly

I enjoy eating healthy foods and drinking water

I enjoy eating green leafy vegetables

My immune system is strong and durable

My organs are healthy

My intestines lungs muscles bones lymphatic system nervousness system organs and skin are in great condition

My mind is attuned to healthy thoughts

My spirit soul radiates vibrantly throughout my body

I listen to my body and its signals

My energy field is cleared

My chakras are cleared and in alignment

My sight, hearing,touch, taste and smell senses are in perfect health

The sun rejuvenates me

I absorb energy from sunlight

I enjoy preparing and eating foods prepared by me

I give thanks for all that I eat and drink

I embody the spirit of power, love and of a sound mind

I take care of my body through good hygiene, proper rest and activeness

My energy is healing, liberating, pleasant and welcoming

CHAPTER 14

THE JOURNALS/ REFLECTIONS

1. In what ways are you currently living in self love?

2. In what ways do you want to increase self love within?

3.In what ways has self love contributed to your well being?

4. Name some ways in how you would help someone else

develop love of self:

5. Why is self love essential?

6. Which affirmations in the chapter of "Self love"

resonates with you the most?

7. Share examples of how self love affects relationships

8. What are your expectations of saying affirmations?

9. How would you define being in the presence of now?

10. What ways do you practice being in the presence now?

11. In what ways have being in the present moment of

now affected your life personally?

12. If someone asked you to explain how you developed being in the present moment of now; how would you respond?

13. What are the disadvantages of not being in the present moment of now?

14. What are the disadvantages of being too focused in the past?

15. What are the disadvantages of being too focused on

the future?

16. Name people places and situations that has helped you

let go of past pains and forgive the past?

17. How has letting go of past pain and forgiving the past benefited you?

18. How can you help others let go of past pain and forgive

the past?

19. What is your perspective on being positive?

20. How would you explain the benefits of a

positive mind versus one of a negative mind set?

21. Give examples of how being in a positive mindset

benefited you ?

22. What does the phrase " living in the positive" mean to you?

23. What testimonials or true life confessions do you have to share with others to uplift and inspire concerning self love?

24. Feel free to write how being in the presence of now has impacted your life?

25. Describe some encounters where you experienced

being in the presence of now?

26. Give testimonials where you have disciplined your mind to remain in the positive?

27. What was your view on the chapter of

"Testimonials/True Story Confessions"?

28. Name some helpful tips involving affirmations that you practice?

29. Which affirmations of positivity caught your attention the most?

30. What are your great I AM's? What are you great in?

31. List below your own personal grateful declarations?

What are you grateful for?What do you declare?

32. What affirmations would you add to the chapter "wholeness and love"?

33. Create and name new affirmations of letting go

34. Why is it important to let go of people places and things that no longer serve your highest good?

35. Why is it important to protect your energy?

36. In what ways do you practice protecting your energy?

37. Why is good health essential to your well being?

38. Give ways in which you practice good health?

39. Give some ideas how someone can improve their

health

40. List symptoms of having good health

ABOUT THE AUTHOR

Angie is an author concerned with the issues of life and solutions to them. Angie has been active in the community as a Certified Teen Advocate assisting teen mothers with counseling and support.. She has great experience as a masseuse with an Associates Degree in Massage Therapy. She is certified in Home Aid Care for the elderly.She has years in Day Care Provision in teaching and monitoring children. Angie is encouraging you to take something from this book and apply it to your life to enhance yourself towards visualizing and thinking thoughts that will propel you into manifesting your desired dreams and desires.

BOOK DESCRIPTION

This is a quick read geared towards training your mind to think healthy and positive thoughts to manifest a healthy and positive reality for yourself. It also deals with factors that determines the way we think as well as habits that assist in healthy thinking resulting in a better reality for yourself.

FROM THE AUTHOR:

My hopes and intentions are that something in this book has enlightened your soul, inspired your mind and encouraged your heart to some degree. Hopefully this book has awakened your awareness of your thoughts, beliefs and perceptions. For it is in the mind where reality is created.

www.ingramcontent.com/pod-product-compliance
Lightning Source LLC
La Vergne TN
LVHW011410080426
835511LV00005B/469